What's Time?

How to Tell Time Explained in Nursery Rhymes

Preetinder Rahil

The author may have checked for errors twice or even thrice, but doing your due diligence would still be considered wise.

As you hear tick and tock,
The noise that comes from a clock.

As you toss and turn in bed,
And listen to what parents have said.

"Get up and go!"
You wish the time could slow.

Isn't it strange?

That all things must change.

What has come must go.
This fact we must all know.

The things we love,

The things we hate,

Time has sealed their fate.

To measure time,

We must have a design.

A clock would do just fine.

The hour hand is short and thick.
The minute hand is longer by a bit.
The second hand is thin like a stick.

It takes sixty clicks for the second hand to turn.

The minute hand moves by one unit in return.

When sixty minutes are done,
The hour hand moves by one.

What' s the time?
If you said eight,
That' s great.

What time does the minute hand show?
Multiplication by five you must know.

After multiplication, we get fifty.
The minute hand is ten minutes away
from twelve, which is equal to minutes sixty.

Clocks are not all alone.

The accuracy of the digital watch has been shown.

The hours are to
the left,
The minutes are
to the right,
Mistakes could
still happen,
But the chances
are only slight.

Which time is easy to read?
If you can't tell,
More practice you'll need.

The digital watch can run quite fast.
Milliseconds are not meant to last.

If you didn't know before,
Each day has hours that are twenty-four.

You may ask why in twenty-four hours the day gets done.
You see, days are designed based on the positions of the sun.

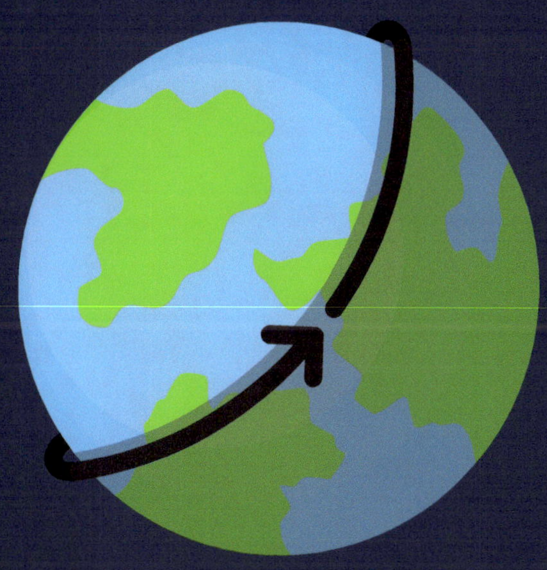

As the earth rotates,
The night becomes day, and the day becomes night.
The sun is never late as it brings the bright light.

| Sun |
| Mon |
| Tue |
| Wed |
| Thu |
| Fri |
| Sat |

There are seven days in a week.

Long weekends we all seek.

Time is flying by even as we speak.

SUN	MON	TUE	WED	THU	FRI	SAT
31					1	2
3	4	5	6	7	8	9
10	11	12	13	14	15	16
17	18	19	20	21	22	23
24	25	26	27	28	29	30

The days in a month are not as simple and straight.

They could be thirty-one, thirty, or even twenty-eight.

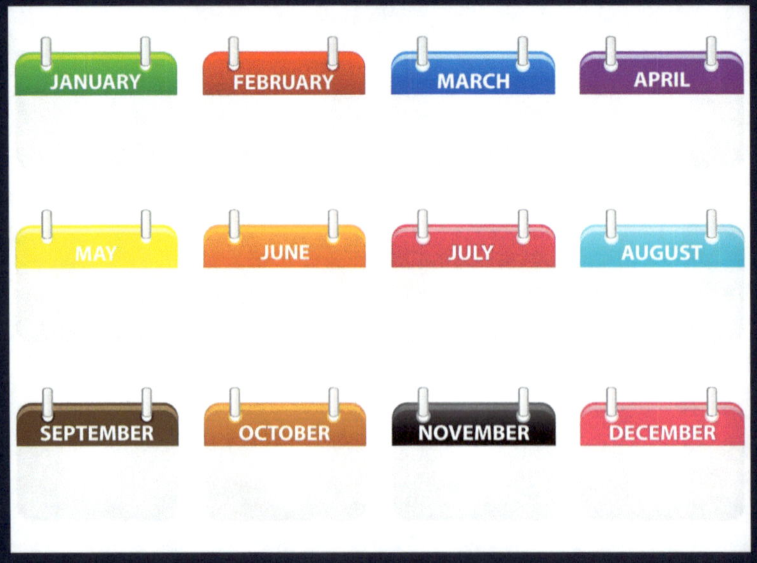

Here's a mnemonic to remember,
Thirty days in September, April, June, and November.

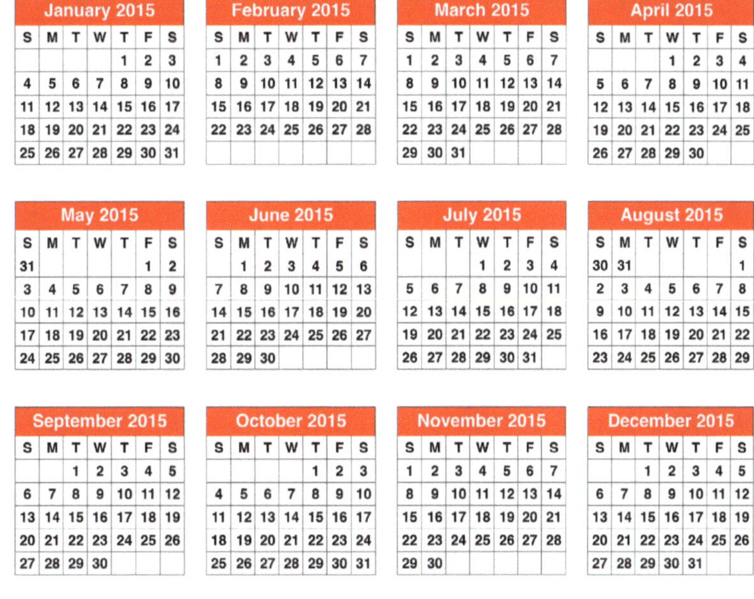

Let me be quite clear,
There are 365 days in a year.

There's another fact to store.

We must add one day more,

As the leap year comes at a yearly interval of four.

With time our memory fades,
As years turn into decades.

There's something magical about the number ten,
A decade is a benchmark for how we lived and when.

Old becomes gold,
As folktales are told,
And centuries unfold.

As present becomes past,
You will realize time moves fast.

But as you'll grow,
You will also know,
Time does get slow.

That's what the theory of relativity says,
As spacetime can be bent in different ways.

Around the black hole, time stands still,
As if each time click must climb a steep hill.

When did the time first start?
We must go to the universe's earliest part.

It's not a guess,
Time started 13.8 billion years ago,
More or less.

Why can't we go back in time?
I don't know about you,
But it has been a dream of mine.

The 2nd law of thermodynamics comes into play.
It keeps the flow of time moving only one way.

It says the number of possibilities must always grow,
And the idea of time travel we must all throw.

In the end, I have only one thing to say.

Times may be good or bad,

But things don't ever stay that way.

Seize each moment,
And live life to the full,
And doing so, be kind and mindful.

About the Author

Preetinder Rahil writes fiction, non-fiction, and poems that rhyme. He tries to keep things simple, fun, and worth your time.